COOKING THE
THE
VIETNAMESE
WAY

This book is available in two editions:
Library binding by Lerner Publications Company,
     a division of Lerner Publishing Group
Soft cover by First Avenue Editions,
     an imprint of Lerner Publishing Group
241 First Avenue North
Minneapolis, MN 55401 U.S.A.

Website address: www.lernerbooks.com

Library of Congress Cataloging-in-Publication Data

Nguyen, Chi.
     Cooking the Vietnamese way / by Chi Nguyen and Judy Monroe.—
Rev. and expanded.
          p. cm. — (Easy menu ethnic cookbooks)
     Includes index.
     ISBN: 0–8225–4125–4 (lib. bdg. : alk. paper)
     ISBN: 0–8225–0513–4 (pbk. : alk. paper)
     1. Cookery, Vietnamese—Juvenile literature. 2. Low-fat
diet—Recipes—Juvenile literature. 3. Vegetarian cookery—
Juvenile literature. [1. Cookery, Vietnamese. 2. Vietnam—Social
life and customs.] I. Monroe, Judy. II. Title. III. Series.
TX724.5.V5 N48 2002
641.59597—dc21   2001002788

Manufactured in the United States of America
1 2 3 4 5 6 – JR – 07 06 05 04 03 02

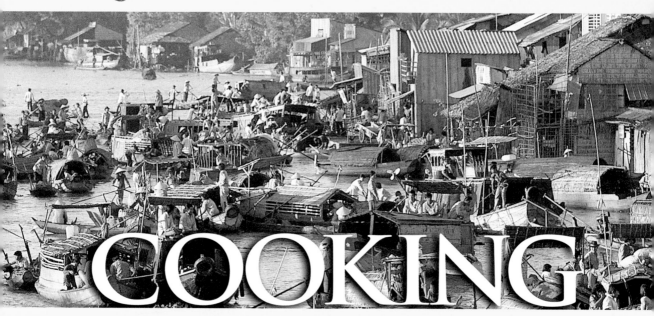

COOKING

revised and expanded

THE

to include new low-fat

VIETNAMESE

and vegetarian recipes

WAY

Chi Nguyen and Judy Monroe

Lerner Publications Company • Minneapolis

Contents

Introduction

Vietnam is an ancient country with deeply rooted traditions. For thousands of years, the Vietnamese people have created beautiful art objects, poetry, and architecture. The same artistic mastery is reflected in the cooking of Vietnam. Freshness and creativity are important characteristics of this great cuisine, which uses colorful ingredients that are carefully prepared and artistically arranged. Many Vietnamese dishes are quite simple to prepare, yet their flavors are satisfying and full of variety.

Despite the fact that Vietnam has been ruled by other countries during its long history, it has also retained its own culture, including its cuisine. Chinese influences are visible in the use of chopsticks for eating and the cooking technique of stir-frying, and the French contributed some of their favorite ingredients to the menu. Nonetheless, the food of Vietnam still has a very distinct character, and cooking the Vietnamese way is a unique and enjoyable experience.

Banh chung *(New Year's Cake) is a favorite dish for Tet (the lunar new year) and is sure to be a winner with your friends and family! (Recipe on page 66.)*

CHINA

Red River

Gulf
of Tonkin

Hanoi
RED
RIVER
DELTA
Haiphong

HAINAN
(CHINA)

LAOS

VIETNAM

TRUONG SON MOUNTAINS

Hue

THAILAND

CAMBODIA
(KAMPUCHEA)

Mekong River

South
China
Sea

Gulf
of Thailand

Ho Chi Minh City

MEKONG
RIVER DELTA

The Land

Vietnam is located south of China in Southeast Asia. The South China Sea surrounds Vietnam to the east and south, with the Gulf of Thailand at Vietnam's southernmost border. To Vietnam's west are the countries of Laos and Cambodia (also known as Kampuchea).

Vietnam is divided into three main land regions: Bac Bo in the north, Trung Bo in the center, and Nam Bo in the south. These three large regions can be further divided into five smaller ones. The northern highlands in northwest Vietnam are covered with jungles and forests. Because the region is so mountainous, it is sparsely populated. The Red River Delta extends south of the northern highlands to the Gulf of Tonkin. The Red River flows across this region into the gulf. This section of Vietnam is highly populated and is also the chief agricultural area in Bac Bo. The central Truong Son Mountains are covered with forests and are not highly populated. From these mountains to the South China Sea are the coastal lowlands. This area produces a great deal of rice, and fishing is a major industry near the coast. The Mekong River forms the Mekong Delta region, and this highly populated area is Vietnam's chief agricultural region.

Most Vietnamese live in the northern and southern regions and along the coast. In Bac Bo, people live in small villages near the rice fields, and the north's two major cities are Hanoi and Haiphong. In Nam Bo, most people live in the Mekong Delta region and in Ho Chi Minh City (formerly Saigon). Trung Bo is quite sparsely populated, and most of its inhabitants live in the city of Hue.

History

Throughout much of its two-thousand-year history, Vietnam has been ruled by other nations. The Chinese conquered Vietnam in the third century B.C. and ruled for one thousand years. Following this period, Vietnam enjoyed nine hundred years of independence. In

1884 France took control of the country. Japan ruled Vietnam for most of World War II (1939–1945), but the French regained control until their defeat in 1954. That year, Vietnam was divided into two separate nations, North Vietnam and South Vietnam.

During the 1960s and 1970s, Vietnam experienced an especially difficult period of war, political unrest, and division. South Vietnam came under Communist rule in 1975, and the Communists unified North and South Vietnam. At that time, thousands of Vietnamese fled their country, and many came to the United States. These refugees brought with them their heritage and their native cuisine. The population of Vietnamese people in other countries, along with the growing number of tourists and visitors to modern Vietnam, have greatly contributed to the popularity of Vietnamese food around the world.

The Food

Because of its warm climate, Vietnam produces an abundance of vegetables and fruits. These fresh ingredients are the mainstays of Vietnamese cuisine. Unlike other Asian cuisines, the Vietnamese serve many uncooked vegetables, often in the form of salads and pickles. Many fresh herbs and spices, including basil, mint, coriander, ginger, chili peppers, and garlic, give Vietnamese food its distinctive flavor and add color to many dishes. Lemon grass, a tropical grass that looks something like scallions, gives food a unique, lemony tang.

Fish and seafood are popular, especially in the central and southern regions. Some of Vietnam's fish is used to make nuoc mam, or fish sauce. The use of fish sauce is a trademark of Vietnamese cooking, and it is the essential ingredient in nuoc cham, a dressing and table sauce that the Vietnamese eat with all foods. Fish sauce is made by combining fish and salt in large barrels and letting it ferment for several months. The golden brown liquid is used as a flavoring ingredient, much like

A Vietnamese woman sells vegetables at an outdoor market in Hanoi.

the Chinese use soy sauce or diners in Europe and the Americas use salt. Fish sauce has a fragrant odor and a subtle taste that combines beautifully with other ingredients.

The Vietnamese include meat in many of their recipes. Pork is the most popular meat, but chicken, duck, and beef are eaten as well. Tofu, or soybean curd, is often used as a high-protein substitute for meat.

Vietnamese cuisine uses several different cooking methods including braising, simmering, steaming, grilling, and stir-frying. Each of these methods preserves and enhances the freshness and flavor of the food. Braising is especially popular, as it requires little heat but produces well-flavored foods in wonderful rich sauces. Little or no oil is used in Vietnamese cooking, even for stir-fried dishes.

The cuisine of Vietnam varies somewhat from region to region. In Bac Bo, fresh produce and herbs are not as widely available as in Trung Bo and Nam Bo, due to the cooler climate. In northern Vietnam, black pepper is the main seasoning. Stir-fried dishes are very popular, probably due to the influence of China, which borders directly to the north. Very hot and spicy food is found in central Vietnam. Southern Vietnam's cooking includes a wide variety of vegetables, fruits, and spices, and sugar is a common ingredient in many dishes. The influence of India is also apparent and curry dishes are very popular. French influence can be found throughout Vietnam, but especially in Nam Bo, where the use of potatoes, asparagus, and even French bread are reminders of France's long presence in Vietnam.

Vietnamese cuisine has been influenced and enriched by the foods and techniques of other countries, but it also draws upon ancient customs and remains unique. As you learn to prepare and enjoy the delicious recipes in this book, you will be carrying on cooking traditions that are thousands of years old.

To many diners who are used to eating with silverware, chopsticks seem like tricky utensils at first. But chopsticks are not difficult to manage once you have learned the basic technique. The key to using them is to hold the inside stick still while moving the outside stick back and forth. The pair then acts as pincers to pick up pieces of food.

Hold the thicker end of the first chopstick in the crook of your thumb, resting the lower part lightly against the inside of your ring finger. Then put the second (outer) chopstick between the tips of your index and middle fingers and hold it with your thumb, much as you would hold a pencil. Now you can make the outer chopstick move by bending your index and middle fingers toward the inside chopstick. The tips of the two sticks should come together like pincers when you bend your fingers. Once you get a feel for the technique, just keep practicing. Soon you'll be an expert!

Holidays and Festivals

The age-old customs and culture carried on by Vietnamese cooking are also reflected in the traditional holidays and festivals of Vietnam. Some of these festivals are based on the beliefs of Buddhism, Confucianism, or Taoism (the three main religions in Vietnam), but all of them can be celebrated and enjoyed by everyone. These events almost always include the preparation of special foods reflecting the nature of the occasion and the time of year. The most joyous and important of these celebrations is Tet Nguyen Dan (often simply called Tet), a festival commemorating the lunar new year and the birth of spring. Like most traditional Vietnamese celebrations, the date of Tet Nguyen Dan is determined by the lunar calendar. The lunar calendar usually has twelve months, each based on the cycle of the moon's revolution around the earth. Every few years, an extra month is added, similar to the practice of adding an extra day in a leap year. Tet falls on the first day of the first lunar month, which can be anywhere between January 21 and February 20.

Although Tet is officially a three-day celebration, during which most businesses, offices, and schools are closed, preparations and festivities usually last for a week or more. The beginning of the holiday season is marked by the departure of the Kitchen Gods. Vietnamese legends describe these three spirits as two men and a woman who watch over the hearth and home and observe all of the family's actions. On the twenty-third night of the twelfth lunar month, the Kitchen Gods leave earth—riding a horse or, according to some of the tales, a carp with golden scales—to report on the family's behavior during the past year. The family prepares special dishes and sends the gods on their way with a farewell feast in the hopes that their report will be a good one.

A crowd of bicyclists and pedestrians, many carrying branches of peach and apricot blossoms, fill streets of an outdoor market before Tet (the lunar new year).

During the next week, Vietnamese families are very busy. Foods must be prepared, gifts must be bought, and homes must be tidied and decorated for this very special holiday. Floors are swept and wood and bronze are brightly polished. Special springtime flowers, such as peach and apricot blossoms, are purchased at outdoor markets and brighten up family homes. Miniature kumquat bushes are also a traditional decoration, representing fertility. The more fruit the bush bears, the more children the family will have. To get the year off to a clean, fresh start, many people buy new clothes, pay old debts, and settle lingering arguments or disputes. The first few days of the new year are believed to set the tone for the rest of the year, so everyone makes a special effort to be positive and to maintain happiness and harmony.

New Year's Eve is a special time, as Vietnamese families gather near the stroke of midnight to pray, light incense, and to invite their deceased ancestors to join them on earth for the Tet festival. A light meal may be served afterward, and the menu often includes a watermelon. The redder the watermelon, the better the luck it promises. The next morning, offerings of food are made to the ancestors, and families, including members who have journeyed home to be together for the holiday, share a delicious feast. The next several days are spent visiting friends and family, exchanging cards and gifts—and, of course, enjoying the many tasty holiday foods that are eaten throughout Tet's celebration.

Each family and region has its own version of banh chung, a special square cake that represents the earth and is made of sticky rice, mung beans, and pork. Some banh chung recipes can take as long as ten or twelve hours to prepare. The cakes are traditionally wrapped in banana leaves and tied together with bamboo. As the cakes boil, Vietnamese cooks prepare a festive dinner made with fresh ingredients of the season, including asparagus soup, stir-fried dishes of crispy new vegetables, and roast suckling pig. A special tray of candied delicacies such as orange, coconut, ginger, lotus seeds, melon, and even flower blossoms is on hand to offer to visitors and guests. Other traditional foods for the new year include a variety of pork dishes, carp, meat and fish pies, and pickled onions.

The Cold Foods Festival, or Tet Han Thuc, takes place on the third day of the third lunar month. This unique festival is held in honor of Gioi Tu Thoi, a loyal subject of a legendary prince who became a proud king. Despite Gioi Tu Thoi's faithful service, he was forgotten by the king and died tragically in a forest fire. In his memory, fire and heat are not used to cook on this day, and only cold foods are eaten. Traditional treats include *banh troi* and *banh chay*, two dishes made with sweet rice flour.

Wandering Souls' Day, or Trung Nguyen, is second only to Tet in importance. The central day of this Buddhist festival, which may last for several weeks, falls on the fifteenth day of the seventh lunar month (usually sometime in August). Most families visit and make offerings at the graves of their own ancestors, but they also honor the spirits of departed souls that have been forgotten or that have no descendants to care for them. During this festival, these souls are said to wander the earth in search of warmth and nourishment, and clothing and food are offered to them at pagodas, temples, and altars all over Vietnam. Fish, meat, and fruit dishes are common offerings to these hungry souls.

The Mid-Autumn Festival, Tet Trung Thu, is another special occasion, falling in the eighth lunar month when the moon is at its fullest and brightest. Originally a celebration of the harvest, this festival is a time to relax after hard work, to admire the beauty of the full moon, and also to pay tribute to the sun for bringing the harvest to fruition.

This celebration is also called the Children's Festival, as children play a special role in the festivities. They parade through the streets wearing masks, performing dances, and carrying glowing lanterns of all shapes and sizes, from spheres and stars to dragons, rabbits, and tigers. At the end of the celebration, these lanterns are set into lakes and rivers to float away in a stream of light. Parents gather their children around them to hear fairy tales and legends, and everyone munches on the traditional moon cakes that are a must at this celebration. These treats are made with a variety of ingredients, from mung beans and sausage to candied lotus seeds and sesame seeds. They may be round like the sun and moon, or in another shape such as a carp (one of the moon's symbols). A wide assortment of fruits is also eaten, and dishes made with snails are another customary delicacy during this festival.

A rich variety of regional celebrations also takes place throughout Vietnam during the year. In Thi Cam village near Hanoi, a rice-cooking festival and contest on January 8 honors Phan Tay Nhac, a heroic military commander. Legends tell of the ingenious leader using such contests to train his soldiers to work together with speed and skill. At the festival, teams are identified by the different colors of their belts as they hurry to fetch water, build and light a fire, and cook pots of steaming white rice. A panel of lucky judges tastes the rice and announces a winner.

A different type of contest—the annual elephant race in Don Village, located in the Truong Son Mountains—draws a large number of spectators in the early spring. Crowds cheer the elephants along and musicians add to the festive atmosphere with drums and gongs, until one speedy elephant wins the race and all of the pachyderm participants enjoy a special snack of sugarcane.

Other festivals around the country involve entertainment and activities such as weaving contests, wrestling, traditional plays, parades, fireworks, singing, and dancing. And, no matter what the event, festivalgoers can always count on a delicious array of foods, from elaborate sit-down feasts to tasty snacks sold by street vendors.

Individual family celebrations are important, too. For example, the Vietnamese do not celebrate birthdays but rather honor departed ancestors on the anniversary of their deaths. For these occasions, food preparations may go on for two days before the celebration. Family tables groan under the weight of foods including roast pig, many kinds of soup, noodle dishes, a variety of side dishes, and several desserts.

Whether a holiday feast or simply an everyday family meal, cooking and eating in Vietnam is always a special occasion in its own right. Vietnamese cooks take great care to prepare dishes that are attractive, nourishing, and, most of all, delicious.

Before You Begin

Vietnamese cooking makes use of some ingredients that you may not know. Sometimes special cookware is used, although the recipes in this book can be prepared with ordinary utensils and pans.

The most important thing you need to know is how to be a careful cook. On the following page, you'll find a few rules that will make your cooking experience safe, fun, and easy. Next, take a look at the "dictionary" of utensils, terms, and ingredients. You may also want to read the list of tips on preparing healthy, low-fat meals.

When you've picked out a recipe, read through it from beginning to end. Now you are ready to shop for ingredients and to organize your cookware. Once you've assembled everything, you're ready to begin cooking. One special feature of Vietnamese cuisine is stir-frying. This cooking technique is very efficient, but it's important to prepare all of your ingredients before you actually start stir-frying. Measure out the spices and herbs, wash fresh vegetables, and do all of the cutting and chopping *before* you heat up the oil. Once the oil is hot, you'll be able to add each ingredient quickly and easily.

Steaming-hot shrimp cakes (recipe on page 65) with nuoc cham (recipe on page 33) make a delicious appetizer or snack.

The Careful Cook

Whenever you cook, there are certain safety rules you must always keep in mind. Even experienced cooks follow these rules when they are in the kitchen.

- Always wash your hands before handling food. Thoroughly wash all raw vegetables and fruits to remove dirt, chemicals, and insecticides. Wash uncooked poultry, fish, and meat under cold water.
- Use a cutting board when cutting up vegetables and fruits. Don't cut them up in your hand! And be sure to cut in a direction *away* from you and your fingers.
- Long hair or loose clothing can easily catch fire if brought near the burners of a stove. If you have long hair, tie it back before you start cooking.
- Turn all pot handles toward the back of the stove so that you will not catch your sleeves or jewelry on them. This is especially important when younger brothers and sisters are around. They could easily knock off a pot and get burned.
- Always use a pot holder to steady hot pots or to take pans out of the oven. Don't use a wet cloth on a hot pan because the steam it produces could burn you.
- Lift the lid of a steaming pot with the opening away from you so that you will not get burned.
- If you get burned, hold the burn under cold running water. Do not put grease or butter on it. Cold water helps to take the heat out, but grease or butter will only keep it in.
- If grease or cooking oil catches fire, throw baking soda or salt at the bottom of the flame to put it out. (Water will *not* put out a grease fire.) Call for help, and try to turn all the stove burners to "off."

Cooking Utensils

colander—A bowl-shaped dish with holes in it that is used for washing or draining food

Dutch oven—A heavy pot, with a tight fitting domed cover, that is often used for cooking soups and stews

skewer—A thin wood, bamboo, or metal stick used to hold small pieces of meat or vegetables for broiling or grilling

steamer—A cooking utensil designed for cooking food with steam. Vietnamese steamers have grates or racks for holding the food and tight fitting lids.

tongs—A two-pronged utensil used to grasp food

wok—A pot with a rounded bottom and sloping sides, ideally suited for stir-frying food. A large skillet is a fine substitute.

Cooking Terms

boil—To heat a liquid over high heat until bubbles form and rise rapidly to the surface

braise—To cook slowly in a covered pot containing liquid

broil—To cook directly under a heat source so that the side of the food facing the heat cooks rapidly

brown—To cook food quickly in fat over high heat so that the surface turns an even brown

garnish—To decorate a dish with herbs or a small piece of food

grate—To shred food into tiny pieces by rubbing it against a grater

grill—To cook food over hot charcoal

marinate—To soak food in liquid to add flavor and to tenderize it

preheat—To allow an oven to warm up to a certain temperature before putting food in it

seed—To remove seeds from a food

shred—To tear or cut into small pieces, either by hand or with a grater

simmer—To cook over low heat in liquid kept just below its boiling point

stir-fry—To cook bite-sized pieces of food quickly in a small amount of oil over high heat

Special Ingredients

black mushrooms—Dried fragrant mushrooms available at Asian groceries. They must be soaked in lukewarm water before using.

cellophane noodles—Thin noodles made from mung beans

coconut milk—The white, milky liquid extracted from coconut meat, used to give a coconut flavor to foods. Canned coconut milk is available at many supermarkets and specialty grocers.

coriander—An herb used as a flavoring and as a decorative garnish. Fresh coriander is also called cilantro.

curry powder—A mixture of several ground spices, such as cayenne pepper and turmeric, that gives food a hot taste

extra-long-grain rice—A type of rice with very large grains. It absorbs more water than other types of rice and is dry and fluffy when cooked.

fish sauce—Called nuoc mam in Vietnamese, this bottled sauce is made from processed fish, water, and salt. It is used widely in Vietnamese cooking and is an ingredient in the sauce nuoc cham. Fish sauce is available at Asian groceries and some supermarkets.

ginger root—A knobby, light brown root used to flavor food

glutinous rice—A short-grain rice that is rather sticky when cooked. Glutinous rice may also be called *sweet rice* or *sticky rice*.

jalapeño peppers—Small, hot green chilies used to give food a spicy flavor

lemon grass—A tropical grass used as a flavoring in Vietnamese food. The lower, white part of the stalk is eaten. Both fresh and dried lemon grass are available in Asian groceries.

lumpia—Thin skins made of flour and water used as wrappers for spring rolls

mung beans—Small beans, usually green in color and often dried, that are widely used in Asian cooking. Mung beans that have been hulled are yellow in color.

red pepper flakes—Dried pieces of hot red peppers used to give a spicy flavor to foods

rice noodles–Long, very thin noodles made from rice flour

sesame seeds—Seeds from an herb grown in tropical countries. They are often toasted before they are eaten.

soy sauce—A sauce made from soybeans and other ingredients that is often used to flavor Asian cooking

tofu—A processed curd made from soybeans

How to Wrap Spring Rolls

1. Have 1 beaten egg and a pastry brush ready.

2. Place about 1½ tbsp. of filling mixture just below center of skin.

3. Fold bottom edge over filling.

4. Fold the two side edges over the filling so that they overlap.

5. Brush top edge corner with beaten egg. Roll up skin toward top edge and press edge to seal. Repeat with remaining wrappers.

Healthy and Low-Fat Cooking Tips

Many modern cooks are concerned about preparing healthy, low-fat meals. Fortunately, there are simple ways to reduce the fat content of most dishes. Here are a few general tips for adapting the recipes in this book. Throughout the book, you'll also find specific suggestions for individual recipes—and don't worry, they'll still taste delicious!

Almost all Vietnamese cooking uses sauces such as fish sauce (nuoc mam), nuoc cham, or soy sauce. Like salt, these seasonings add a great deal of flavor but are high in sodium. To lower the sodium content of these dishes, you may simply reduce how much of these sauces you use. You can also substitute low-sodium soy sauce for the regular variety. Be aware that soy sauce labeled "light" is usually actually lighter in color than regular soy sauce, not lower in sodium.

Many Vietnamese dishes include meat or fish. However, it is easy to adapt most of the recipes in this book to be vegetarian. Tofu (a soybean product) and mock duck (a wheat product) both make simple and satisfying substitutions for meat. Or try substituting extra vegetables, especially hardy vegetables like mushrooms, potatoes, or eggplant.

Some recipes call for oil to sauté vegetables or other ingredients. Reducing the amount of oil you use is one quick way to reduce fat. You can also substitute a low-fat or nonfat cooking spray for oil. Sprinkling just a little bit of salt on vegetables brings out their natural juices, so less oil is needed. It's also a good idea to use a nonstick frying pan if you decide to use less oil than the recipe calls for.

There are many ways to prepare meals that are good for you and still taste great. As you become a more experienced cook, try experimenting with recipes and substitutions to find the methods that work best for you.

METRIC CONVERSIONS

Cooks in the United States measure both liquid and solid ingredients using standard containers based on the 8-ounce cup and the tablespoon. These measurements are based on volume, while the metric system of measurement is based on both weight (for solids) and volume (for liquids). To convert from U.S. fluid tablespoons, ounces, quarts, and so forth to metric liters is a straightforward conversion, using the chart below. However, since solids have different weights—one cup of rice does not weigh the same as one cup of grated cheese, for example—many cooks who use the metric system have kitchen scales to weigh different ingredients. The chart below will give you a good starting point for basic conversions to the metric system.

MASS (weight)

1 ounce (oz.)	= 28.0 grams (g)
8 ounces	= 227.0 grams
1 pound (lb.) or 16 ounces	= 0.45 kilograms (kg)
2.2 pounds	= 1.0 kilogram

LIQUID VOLUME

1 teaspoon (tsp.)	= 5.0 milliliters (ml)
1 tablespoon (tbsp.)	= 15.0 milliliters
1 fluid ounce (oz.)	= 30.0 milliliters
1 cup (c.)	= 240 milliliters
1 pint (pt.)	= 480 milliliters
1 quart (qt.)	= 0.95 liters (l)
1 gallon (gal.)	= 3.80 liters

LENGTH

¼ inch (in.)	= 0.6 centimeters (cm)
½ inch	= 1.25 centimeters
1 inch	= 2.5 centimeters

TEMPERATURE

212°F	= 100°C (boiling point of water)
225°F	= 110°C
250°F	= 120°C
275°F	= 135°C
300°F	= 150°C
325°F	= 160°C
350°F	= 180°C
375°F	= 190°C
400°F	= 200°C

(To convert temperature in Fahrenheit to Celsius, subtract 32 and multiply by .56)

PAN SIZES

8-inch cake pan	= 20 x 4-centimeter cake pan
9-inch cake pan	= 23 x 3.5-centimeter cake pan
11 x 7-inch baking pan	= 28 x 18-centimeter baking pan
13 x 9-inch baking pan	= 32.5 x 23-centimeter baking pan
9 x 5-inch loaf pan	= 23 x 13-centimeter loaf pan
2-quart casserole	= 2-liter casserole

A Vietnamese Table

Most Vietnamese kitchens are rich in ingredients, spices, and time-honored recipes, yet have a minimum of special utensils and fancy cookware. Similarly, the typical Vietnamese table is set simply, usually with only a bowl, a small dipping saucer (often used for nuoc cham), and chopsticks at each place. Most of the food is served in communal dishes, and diners are free to help themselves to whatever they like. At banquets and special occasions, the table may be set more elaborately. More courses are generally served and the seating arrangement is more formal, usually with the head or elder of the family or group sitting in the first seat, closest to the family altar.

The most important elements of any Vietnamese meal are the food and the company. The evening meal is a favorite time for families and friends to gather. The freshest vegetables, seafood, and meats available are presented in a selection of delicious and attractive dishes, and everyone enjoys a good meal and a good conversation.

Eating at outdoor restaurants is common in Vietnam, which has a warm, tropical climate.

A Vietnamese Menu

The Vietnamese serve three meals a day, plus snacks of fruit and clear soups. Breakfast, lunch, and dinner dishes are often interchangeable, although breakfast tends to be a lighter meal. Rice is served at every meal, and nuoc cham is always on the table.

Below are menu plans for a typical Vietnamese lunch and dinner, along with shopping lists of the ingredients to prepare these meals. When planning any Vietnamese meal, remember that harmony and balance are key concepts, though contrasts are important, too. For instance, hot and cold dishes are served together, a spicy dish is eaten with bland rice, and a light soup might be teamed with an elaborate steamed dish.

LUNCH

Sweet and sour soup

Shredded chicken-cabbage salad

Rice

Tea

Nuoc cham

SHOPPING LIST:

Produce

3 tomatoes
3 scallions
1 small head of cabbage
2 limes
1 bulb garlic
fresh mint
fresh coriander

Dairy/Egg/Meat

1 lb. fish fillets
2 boneless skinless chicken
  breasts

Canned/Bottled/Boxed

vegetable oil
2 10¾-oz. cans chicken
  broth
1 20-oz. can chunk
  pineapple
white vinegar
roasted peanuts
fish sauce

Miscellaneous

rice
loose tea
black pepper
sugar
salt
cayenne pepper
red pepper flakes

DINNER

Shrimp salad

Spring rolls

Braised chicken

Fried rice

Tea

Nuoc cham

SHOPPING LIST:

Produce

1 cucumber
7 carrots
2 limes
1 jalapeño pepper
2 medium onions
2 scallions
½ c. fresh or frozen peas
fresh coriander
fresh ginger
1 bulb garlic

Dairy/Egg/Meat

3 eggs
1 lb. fresh or frozen shrimp
1 lb. lean ground pork
8 chicken thighs or legs

Canned/Bottled/Boxed

3½-oz. package cellophane
    or rice noodles
1-lb. package lumpia
vegetable oil
fish sauce
soy sauce
white vinegar

Miscellaneous

sesame seeds
red pepper flakes
black pepper
salt
sugar
rice
loose tea

*If you plan to do a lot of Vietnamese cooking, you may
want to stock up on some of the items on these shopping lists
and keep them on hand. Rice, fish sauce, soy sauce, and tea all
keep well and are used to prepare most Vietnamese meals.

Vietnamese Staples

Steaming bowls of rice are on the table at all Vietnamese meals, no matter how simple or light. More than ten varieties of rice are available in Vietnam, and products made from rice range from flour and noodles to vinegar and wine. Purchasing rice, usually from a local grocer or dealer, is an important transaction for Vietnamese cooks, and wasting rice for any reason is definitely in bad taste.

Nuoc cham is almost as important to the Vietnamese diet as rice and is just as common on the Vietnamese table. Made from a base of nuoc mam, a strong fish sauce, nuoc cham is used alone for dipping and also as an ingredient in cooking.

Tea is also a central part of Vietnamese culture. Not all diners drink tea with meals, but no social gathering would be complete without it, and it is enjoyed throughout the day, alone or with snacks. The Vietnamese drink both green and black teas, and tea flavored with flowers such as jasmine or lotus is especially popular.

Rice noodles (recipe on page 32) and nuoc cham (recipe on page 33) are two staples of Vietnamese cuisine.

Rice/ *Com*

2 c. extra-long-grain white rice

2½ c. water

1. In a deep saucepan, bring rice and water to a boil over high heat. Boil uncovered 2 to 3 minutes.

2. Cover pan and turn heat to low. Simmer rice 20 to 25 minutes, or until all water is absorbed.

3. Remove from heat. Cover and let rice steam for 10 minutes.

4. Fluff rice with a fork and serve hot.

Cooking time: 35 to 45 minutes
Serves 4

Rice Noodles/ *Bun*

Rice noodles, also called rice sticks, may be added to soups or to stir-fried, steamed, or simmered dishes. They are sometimes served cold with hot vegetables and meat on top of them.

3 c. water

1 7-oz. package rice noodles

1. In a large saucepan, bring water to a boil over high heat. Add rice noodles and return water to a boil.

2. Reduce heat to medium-high and cook noodles uncovered for 4 to 5 minutes, or until soft.

3. Drain and rinse noodles in a colander. Serve immediately.

Cooking time: 10 minutes
Serves 4

Nuoc Cham

The Vietnamese use nuoc cham the way diners in many countries use salt. It is included on every table for every meal, either as a dip or a sauce to pour over a dish, and it is usually served in individual bowls. Drained carrot salad is often added to nuoc cham.

2 cloves garlic, crushed

1 tsp. red pepper flakes

3 tbsp. sugar

2 tbsp. fresh lime juice or 4 tbsp. white vinegar

4 tbsp. fish sauce

1 c. water

1. Combine all ingredients in a small mixing bowl. Stir to dissolve sugar. (If sauce is too salty or too strong, add another tablespoon of water and stir well.)

Preparation time: 5 to 10 minutes
Makes 1½ cups

*Nuoc cham will keep for up to two weeks if it is refrigerated in a tightly covered glass container.

Carrot Salad/ Goi co rot

Carrot salad can be eaten plain with any meal, or it can be added to nuoc cham. It can be kept in the refrigerator for two or three days if stored in its liquid.

2 c. water

4 tbsp. white vinegar

2 tbsp. sugar

1 tsp. salt

4 to 5 carrots

1. In a small bowl, combine water, vinegar, sugar, and salt. Stir until sugar and salt are dissolved.

2. Peel the carrots and shred finely with a grater.

3. Pour liquid over shredded carrot. Cover and refrigerate overnight.

4. Drain salad in a colander. Serve at room temperature in individual bowls.

Preparation time: 10 minutes
Chilling time: overnight
Serves 4

*For a variation on this simple salad, try adding about 1 c. grated Asian radish (also called daikon) to the mixture.

Carrot salad adds a splash of color—and flavor—to any meal.

Soups and Salads

Soup is included with almost every Vietnamese meal, often served over rice and garnished with coriander. Pho, a noodle soup that has many variations, is almost a national dish in Vietnam and is especially popular as a hearty breakfast dish. The wide variety of different Vietnamese soups, some thin and delicate, others hearty and thick, presents diners with delicious choices.

Salads are another important and unique part of the Vietnamese cuisine. The Vietnamese treasure fresh, crunchy vegetables such as lettuce, cucumbers, and carrots, and seasonal specialties. Simple but tasty dressings enhance the flavors of each ingredient, and salads are often garnished with fresh mint leaves or fresh coriander. Meat, seafood, or noodles may be added as well, making a salad as light or as substantial as the cook desires.

Sesame seeds and fresh coriander dress up a dish of shrimp salad. (Recipe on page 39.)

Sweet and Sour Soup/ *Canh chua ca*

This soup combines the sweetness of pineapple with the sour taste of vinegar. The pineapple, native to Vietnam, is considered a vegetable in that country.

1 lb. fish fillets, cut into bite-sized pieces*

¼ tsp. pepper

2 tbsp. oil

3 tomatoes, cut into 8 wedges each

1 tsp. sugar

2 10¾-oz. cans (about 3 c.) chicken broth

1 20-oz. can chunk pineapple, drained thoroughly

2 tbsp. white vinegar

2 tbsp. chopped fresh mint leaves or 1 tsp. dried mint

¼ c. chopped scallions

1. In a large mixing bowl, mix together fish and pepper. Cover and let stand at room temperature for 30 minutes.

2. In a large saucepan, heat oil over medium heat for 2 minutes. Add tomatoes and sugar. Cook 2 minutes, or until tomatoes are soft.

3. Add chicken broth, pineapple, and fish. Bring to a boil over high heat. Reduce heat to medium and simmer for 5 minutes, or until fish is cooked through and tender.

4. Add vinegar, mint, and scallions.

5. Serve over hot rice or in individual soup bowls with rice on the side.

Preparation time: 45 minutes
Cooking time: 25 minutes
Serves 4

*For this soup, you can use fresh or frozen sole, cod, or haddock fillets. If you use frozen fish, thaw completely before using.

Shrimp Salad / Goi tom

1 cucumber, peeled and chopped

3 carrots, peeled and grated

2 tsp. sugar

3 c. water

1 lb. fresh shrimp, peeled and deveined*, or 1 lb. frozen shrimp, thawed

2 tbsp. fish sauce

2 tsp. lime juice or white vinegar

1 jalapeño pepper, seeded and chopped, or ½ tsp. red pepper flakes

1 tbsp. sesame seeds

fresh coriander for garnish (optional)

*If you use fresh shrimp for this recipe, you may be able to have it peeled and deveined at the grocery store. Otherwise, you can do it yourself. Hold the shrimp so that the underside is facing you. Starting at the head, use your fingers to peel off the shell from the head toward the tail. Then, using a sharp knife, carefully make a shallow cut all the way down the middle of the back. Hold the shrimp under cold running water to rinse out the dark vein.

1. In a large mixing bowl, combine cucumber, carrots, and 1 tsp. sugar. Cover and let stand at room temperature for 15 minutes.

2. In a large saucepan, bring 3 c. water to a boil over high heat. Add shrimp and boil 3 to 4 minutes, or until tender, bright pink, and curled tightly. Drain well in a colander and set aside in a covered dish.

3. Place cucumber-carrot mixture in a colander and drain well. Return to mixing bowl. Add shrimp and stir.

4. In a small bowl, combine 1 tsp. sugar, fish sauce, lime juice, and pepper. Stir well and pour over shrimp and vegetable mixture.

5. Place sesame seeds in a small skillet without oil. Cook 1 to 3 minutes over medium heat, stirring frequently until seeds are golden. Set pan aside.

6. Place salad on a serving plate and sprinkle with toasted sesame seeds. Garnish with fresh coriander and serve cold or at room temperature.

Preparation time: 25 minutes
Cooking time: 25 to 30 minutes
Serves 4

Shredded Chicken-Cabbage Salad/ Goi ga

On special occasions, the Vietnamese start the meal with a salad such as this shredded chicken-cabbage salad. For a regular family-style meal, all dishes, including the salad, are served at once.

2 whole chicken breasts, skinned

½ small head cabbage, shredded
(about 2 c.)

juice of 1 lime*

½ tsp. salt

⅛ tsp. cayenne pepper

¼ c. chopped roasted peanuts
(optional)

fresh coriander for garnish
(optional)

* This salad is also delicious served with nuoc cham (page 33) in place of the lime juice dressing.

1. Rinse chicken breasts under cool running water and pat dry with paper towels.

2. Place chicken in a large saucepan with enough water to cover. Bring to a boil. Turn heat to low, cover pan, and simmer for 30 minutes.

3. Remove chicken from pan with tongs. Place on a plate and cool for 15 minutes. When chicken is cool, remove meat from bones and shred into small pieces.

4. Place shredded chicken in a large bowl and add shredded cabbage.

5. In another small bowl, mix lime juice, salt, and cayenne pepper.

6. Pour lime juice mixture over chicken and cabbage. Mix thoroughly.

7. Place salad on a serving plate and garnish with peanuts and coriander. Serve at room temperature.

Preparation time: 10 minutes
Cooking time: 1 hour
Serves 4

Rice Noodle Salad/Bun bo sao

This salad is a meal in itself. The combination of hot and cold ingredients and the contrast between crunchy vegetables and soft noodles and meat make this a favorite dish throughout Vietnam, where it is eaten primarily in the summer.

1 7-oz. package rice noodles

½ medium head lettuce, shredded (about 2 c.)

½ cucumber, peeled and thinly sliced

2 carrots, peeled and shredded

2 tbsp. vegetable oil

½ onion, peeled and thinly sliced

1 lb. pork loin or beef sirloin tip, thinly sliced

1 stem lemon grass, finely chopped, or 1 tbsp. dried lemon grass*

1 clove garlic, finely chopped

½ tsp. sugar

¼ tsp. pepper

2 tbsp. fish sauce

½ c. chopped roasted peanuts

1. Cook and drain noodles (see recipe on page 32). When the noodles are cool, use a sharp knife or scissors to cut noodles into shorter lengths.

2. Divide rice noodles among 4 small bowls. Divide lettuce, cucumber, and carrot and add to each bowl. Set aside.

3. In a large skillet, heat oil over high heat for 1 minute. Add onion and cook, stirring frequently, for 2 to 3 minutes, or until tender.

4. Add meat and stir. Add lemon grass, garlic, sugar, and pepper. Cook, stirring frequently, 3 to 5 minutes, or until meat is thoroughly cooked. Add fish sauce and stir well.

5. Divide cooked meat mixture among the four bowls and sprinkle 2 tbsp. peanuts over each.

6. Serve with nuoc cham (page 33).

Preparation time: 20 minutes
Cooking time: 30 to 35 minutes
Serves 4

*Before using dried lemon grass, place it in a dish of hot water and allow it to soak for 30 minutes to an hour. Drain well and chop finely.

Quick-Cooked Dishes

The Vietnamese enjoy stir-fried dishes because this efficient quick-cooking method produces crunchy vegetables and tender, flavorful meat. Before stir-frying, be sure to have all of your ingredients prepared and within reach. Fried treats such as spring rolls are also a favorite snack or appetizer. Vietnamese cooks usually use woks for stir-frying and frying, but French influence has made the use of ordinary skillets quite common, too.

Grilling is another important Vietnamese cooking method. In Vietnamese homes, food is grilled over a fire on the kitchen floor and then brought to the table. Outside, street vendors with small grills often sell treats to hungry passersby. With the help of an experienced cook, you can use a charcoal or gas grill for the grilled dishes in this book. Your broiler will also work just fine.

This basic recipe for fried rice combines vegetables, cooked rice, and scrambled eggs, but you can vary the dish with your favorite ingredients. (Recipe on page 46.)

Fried Rice / *Com chien*

Fried rice originated in China. This version, flavored with fish sauce, is uniquely Vietnamese. It is a great way to use up leftovers, since just about any kind of meat or vegetable can be added.

2 eggs

4 tbsp. vegetable oil

½ medium onion, chopped

I carrot, chopped

½ c. fresh green peas or frozen peas, thawed

½ tsp. pepper

I tsp. sugar

2 tsp. fish sauce

I tsp. soy sauce

4 c. cold cooked rice

1. In a small bowl, beat eggs well.

2. In a large skillet, heat 1 tbsp. oil over medium heat for 1 minute. Add beaten eggs and cook quickly, scrambling them with a spoon. Place eggs on a plate and set aside.

3. In a clean skillet, heat 3 tbsp. oil over medium heat for 1 minute. Add onions and cook uncovered for 2 minutes, stirring occasionally. Add carrots and peas, stir well, and cook 5 minutes, covered.

4. Add pepper, sugar, fish sauce, and soy sauce and stir well.

5. Add rice, breaking apart any clumps. Mix well and cook uncovered 7 to 8 minutes, or until heated through.

6. Just before serving, add scrambled eggs and mix well. Serve hot.

Preparation time: 10 minutes
Cooking time: 30 to 40 minutes
Serves 4

Stir-fried Beef with Green Beans/ *Thit bo sao dau*

1 clove garlic, finely chopped

¼ tsp. pepper

1 tsp. cornstarch or flour

1 tsp. vegetable oil

1 lb. sirloin tips, thinly sliced

3 tbsp. vegetable oil

½ medium onion, sliced

2 c. green beans, with ends removed and cut into bite-sized pieces*

¼ c. water or chicken broth

1 tsp. soy sauce

* This typical family dish can be made with chopped celery, broccoli, or cauliflower in place of the green beans. For a delicious vegetarian dish, try replacing the beef with tofu or hardy vegetables such as eggplant or mushrooms.

1. In a large mixing bowl, combine garlic, pepper, cornstarch, and 1 tsp. oil. Add beef and mix well. Cover and let stand at room temperature for 30 minutes.

2. In a wok or large skillet, heat 2 tbsp. oil over high heat for 1 minute. Add meat. Stir quickly over high heat for about 2 minutes, or until beef begins to turn brown. Remove from pan and place in a large bowl. Set aside.

3. Wash wok or skillet and dry well.

4. Heat 1 tbsp. oil over high heat for 1 minute. Add onion and cook, stirring frequently, for 2 minutes, or until nearly tender.

5. Add green beans and stir well. Add water or broth, cover, and turn heat to low. Simmer for 4 to 5 minutes, or until beans are tender but crisp.

6. Uncover and add soy sauce and beef. Cook over medium heat for 1 to 2 minutes, stirring constantly, until heated through.

7. Serve over hot rice.

Preparation and standing time: 40 to 45 minutes
Cooking time: 20 minutes
Serves 4

Stir-fried Cauliflower/*Bong cai*

Cauliflower was introduced by the French in the 1800s. Because it looks like a big flower and is from the cabbage family, the Vietnamese call cauliflower "the flower of the cabbage."

1 medium head cauliflower*

1 tbsp. vegetable oil

1 small onion, sliced

½ tsp. pepper

1 tbsp. fish sauce

¼ c. chopped scallions

1. Break cauliflower into bite-sized florets.

2. In a large skillet or wok, heat oil over high heat for 1 minute.

3. Add onion and cook over high heat, stirring constantly, for 3 minutes, or until onion is tender.

4. Add cauliflower. Cook 2 to 3 minutes, stirring constantly. Add pepper and fish sauce and mix well. Cover and cook another 2 minutes, or until cauliflower is tender but not mushy.

5. Add scallions and stir. Serve hot with rice.

Preparation time: 5 minutes
Cooking time: 10 to 12 minutes
Serves 4

*You can easily substitute any chopped vegetable for the cauliflower in this dish. Or, try combining an assortment of vegetables for extra variety.

This simple stir-fry can be a delicious side dish or a main course.

Spring Rolls/ *Cha gio*

These crispy, delicious treats make a great start to any meal.

3½ oz. (one-half package)
cellophane or rice noodles

I egg

I lb. ground pork

3 carrots, peeled and shredded

I small onion, chopped

1½ tsp. fish sauce

½ tsp. pepper

¼ cup chopped scallions

I I-lb. package lumpia, thawed
(about 25 wrappers)*

½ c. vegetable oil

* Look for lumpia in specialty
groceries.

1. Soak noodles in hot water according to package directions. When soft, drain and cut into 2-inch lengths with a sharp knife or scissors.

2. In a large bowl, beat egg well. Add noodles, pork, carrots, onion, fish sauce, pepper, and scallions. Mix well.

3. Place one wrapper on a flat surface. Cover remaining wrappers with a slightly damp kitchen towel so they don't dry out. Roll up according to directions on page 23.

4. In a large skillet or wok, heat oil over medium heat for 1 minute. Carefully place 3 rolls into oil and fry slowly about 10 minutes, or until golden brown. Turn and fry other side 10 minutes.

5. Keep fried rolls warm in a 200°F oven as you fry remaining rolls.

6. Serve hot with individual bowls of nuoc cham for dipping. Cut each spring roll into 4 pieces, or wrap spring roll plus a few sprigs of fresh mint and coriander in a lettuce leaf, dip, and eat.

Preparation time: 1½ to 2 hours
Cooking time: 2 to 3 hours
Makes about 25 spring rolls

Grilled Lemon Grass Beef/Bo nuong xa

Grilled lemon grass beef is usually served at summer picnics and is always popular at parties and celebrations. This is a southern specialty. Cooks in northern Vietnam usually grill pork instead of beef.

1½ lb. sirloin tip, thinly sliced

2 tsp. sugar

2 tbsp. soy sauce

1 tsp. pepper

2 cloves garlic, finely chopped

2 tsp. sesame seeds

2 stems lemon grass, finely chopped, or 2 tbsp. dried lemon grass, soaked

12 romaine lettuce leaves (optional)

2 tsp. each chopped fresh mint, coriander, and scallions (optional)

1. Mix sirloin, sugar, soy sauce, pepper, garlic, sesame seeds, and lemon grass in a large mixing bowl. Cover and refrigerate 4 hours or overnight.

2. Soak 12 small wooden skewers in water until ready to use.

3. Preheat oven to broil or have an experienced cook help you start a charcoal grill.

4. Thread beef slices onto skewers accordion-style. When oven is preheated or charcoal ready, broil or grill beef for 6 to 8 minutes, or until done, turning often so that all sides are cooked evenly.

5. Serve hot from skewers or remove meat from a skewer and place on a lettuce leaf. Add ½ tsp. each of chopped fresh mint, coriander, and scallions. Roll up leaf, dip in nuoc cham, and serve.

Preparation time: 30 to 35 minutes
Chilling time: 4 hours to overnight
Cooking time: 6 to 8 minutes
Serves 4

Slow-Cooked Dishes

Braising is the most popular cooking method for meat in Vietnam. This slow-cooking method produces tender meat in savory sauces. It is an especially good method for cooking tougher cuts of meats.

Simmered dishes are cooked slowly at a temperature just below boiling. Flavors have a chance to mingle, and dishes are always moist. In Vietnam, braising and simmering are usually done over charcoal, but the top of your stove will work just as well.

The Vietnamese menu also includes many dishes that are steamed or cooked over boiling water. This method keeps food tasting fresh and looking attractive and also helps food retain most of its nutrients. If you don't have a metal steamer, set a heat-resistant bowl containing the food to be steamed into a flat pan. Pour about ½ c. of boiling water into the pan. Cover the bowl, and place the pan and the dish in a preheated 350°F oven for the amount of time specified in the recipe.

Serve braised chicken (recipe on page 56) with sticky rice with corn and coconut (recipe on page 57) for a tasty and elegant meal.

Braised Chicken / Ga kho gung

If you are served chicken in Vietnam, you know you are well liked, as chicken there is rather expensive. This particular chicken dish is also served to new mothers as a special treat and to help restore their strength. Dark-meat chicken is especially good for braising, but white meat is fine, too.

1 tbsp. finely chopped fresh ginger

¼ tsp. salt

¼ tsp. pepper

8 chicken thighs or legs, skinned*

2 tbsp. vegetable oil

½ small onion, chopped

2 c. water

1 tsp. sugar

2 tbsp. fish sauce

1. In a small bowl, mix ginger, salt, and pepper. Rub mixture into chicken pieces and cover. Let stand at room temperature for 30 minutes.

2. In a large skillet, heat oil over high heat for 1 minute. Add onion and cook uncovered for 2 to 3 minutes, or until tender. Stir frequently.

3. Add chicken, water, sugar, and fish sauce. Cover and reduce heat to low. Simmer for 45 minutes, or until chicken is tender.

4. Serve hot with rice or noodles.

Preparation time: 45 minutes
Cooking time: 1¼ to 1½ hours
Serves 4

*After handling raw chicken or other poultry, always remember to thoroughly wash your hands, utensils, and preparation area with soapy hot water. Also, when checking chicken for doneness, it's a good idea to cut it open gently to make sure that the meat is white (not pink) all the way through.

Sticky Rice with Corn and Coconut/ ʃɔi dua

Sticky rice, also known as glutinous or sweet rice, is a kind of short-grain rice. When cooked, it is quite sticky and can be molded into shapes. You may substitute any chopped vegetable for the corn and regular short-grain rice can substitute for the glutinous rice.

3 c. water

2 c. glutinous rice

1 8-oz. can corn, drained well

1 c. canned coconut milk* or whole milk

2 tsp. salt

4 tsp. sugar

¼ c. sesame seeds

½ c. chopped roasted peanuts

Look for "lite" coconut milk at the grocery store. While it doesn't have the same creamy consistency of regular coconut milk, it has all the flavor and far fewer calories and grams of fat.

1. In a large saucepan, bring water and rice to a boil over high heat. Turn heat to low and cover. Simmer for 20 to 25 minutes, or until water is absorbed and rice is tender.

2. Add corn, coconut milk, 1 tsp. salt, and 2 tsp. sugar and mix well. Cover and keep warm over very low heat.

3. Place sesame seeds in a small skillet (do not add oil). Turn heat to medium and cook seeds about 2 to 3 minutes, or until they begin to turn a light golden color. Stir frequently, being careful not to let seeds burn. When seeds are golden, pour into a small mixing bowl.

4. Add 1 tsp. salt, 2 tsp. sugar, and peanuts to sesame seeds. Mix well.

5. Spoon rice mixture into individual bowls. Sprinkle 2 to 3 tsp. of peanut-sesame seed mixture over each bowl of rice. Serve hot, cold, or at room temperature.

Preparation time: 5 minutes
Cooking time: 40 to 55 minutes
Serves 4

Sweet Potatoes with Peanuts/ *Khoai lang nau*

2 c. water

½ c. sugar

2 medium sweet potatoes, peeled and cut into chunks

½ tsp. salt

¼ tsp. pepper

¼ c. chopped roasted peanuts

1. In a large saucepan, bring water and sugar to a boil over high heat.

2. Add sweet potatoes and cover. Turn heat to low and simmer for 10 minutes, or until tender.

3. In a colander, drain sweet potatoes and place in a serving bowl. Add salt and pepper and stir. Sprinkle with peanuts and serve hot.

Preparation time: 5 to 10 minutes
Cooking time: 20 to 25 minutes
Serves 4

Steamed Tofu/ *Dau hui hap*

1 lb. firm tofu, cut into chunks*

2 tbsp. soy sauce

½ c. chopped scallions

¼ tsp. salt

¼ tsp. pepper

¼ tsp. red pepper flakes

1. Place all ingredients in a heat-resistant bowl and mix well.

2. Place ½ c. water in steamer and bring to a boil over high heat. Place bowl with tofu into steamer. Cover and steam over medium heat for 25 minutes.

3. Serve hot, with rice or alone.

Preparation time: 10 to 15 minutes
Cooking time: 35 to 40 minutes
Serves 4

Sweet potatoes with peanuts (top) is a common breakfast dish in southern Vietnam. Tofu (bottom) is a good source of protein for vegetarians.

Steamed Fish / *Ca hap*

With its long coastline and many rivers, Vietnam enjoys an abundance of fresh fish, and seafood is an important part of the menu. For this recipe, you can use sole, cod, haddock, or any other white fish. If you use frozen fish, thaw thoroughly before mixing with the other ingredients.

2 lb. fish fillets, cut into bite-sized pieces

2 tsp. fish sauce

⅛ tsp. pepper

1 clove garlic, chopped

1 tsp. finely chopped fresh ginger

½ c. sliced fresh mushrooms

3 stalks celery, cut into chunks

1 tomato, cut into chunks

¼ c. chopped scallions

1. Place all ingredients in a heat-resistant bowl and mix well.

2. Place ½ c. water in steamer and bring to a boil over high heat. Place bowl with fish mixture into steamer. Cover and steam over medium heat for 40 minutes.

3. Serve hot with rice. Spoon juices over fish and rice.

Preparation time: 25 to 30 minutes
Cooking time: 45 to 55 minutes
Serves 4

Fresh ginger and garlic give a bit of zip to this tasty seafood dish.

Holiday and Festival Food

Eating is always an enjoyable event in Vietnam, but during festivals and special occasions, food takes on added importance. Cooks prepare their most prized recipes, whether their own creations or traditional favorites. They pay close attention to make sure that everything looks as wonderful as it tastes.

As always, family meals are a special time during the holidays. More people at the table only make the occasion more joyful, as relatives and friends may have traveled from far away to be together for the celebration. Serving a large holiday meal or a banquet may be extra work. But most Vietnamese cooks take pride in their art and enjoy making their best dishes at home rather than buying foods already prepared. On a festival day, or any day, carrying on the cooking traditions of past generations is a fun part of celebrating Vietnamese culture and cuisine.

Delicate, creamy asparagus soup makes a wonderful beginning to a holiday meal. (Recipe on page 64.)

Asparagus Soup/ Súp mang

Since asparagus is best in the early spring, this soup is a favorite choice during Tet Nguyen Dan. Asparagus was brought to Vietnam by the French and quickly became a very popular vegetable. The Vietnamese call asparagus Western bamboo because it looks similar to bamboo shoots.

1 egg

2 tbsp. cornstarch

¼ c. water

2 10¾-oz. cans (about 3 c.) chicken broth

½ lb. fresh asparagus, cut into bite-sized pieces, or 1 10-oz. package frozen chopped asparagus, thawed

1 whole chicken breast, skinned, boned, and cut into bite-sized pieces*

2 tsp. fish sauce

For a dressier holiday dish, substitute 8 ounces of cooked crab meat for the chicken in this recipe.

1. Beat egg in a small bowl. Set aside.

2. In another small bowl, mix cornstarch and water to make a paste. Set aside.

3. In a large saucepan, bring broth to a boil over high heat. Add asparagus and reduce heat to medium. Cover and cook for 3 minutes, or until tender but still crisp.

4. Add chicken. Cook for 3 to 4 minutes, or until chicken and asparagus are thoroughly cooked.

5. Add fish sauce and cornstarch paste. (If cornstarch has started to separate from the water, stir well before adding.) Stir well for about 1 to 2 minutes, or until soup starts to thicken.

6. Add beaten egg a little at a time, stirring constantly. Cook for 30 seconds.

7. Serve hot over rice, or in individual soup bowls with rice on the side.

Preparation time: 20 minutes
Cooking time: 25 to 30 minutes
Serves 4

Shrimp Cakes/Banh tom

Street vendors sell hot, tasty snacks at events and celebrations around Vietnam. Hungry festival-goers never have to look far for a treat. Shrimp cakes are a favorite that can also be made at home.

I lb. fresh or frozen shrimp, peeled and deveined*

1½ c. flour

1½ c. water

1¼ c. salt

⅛ tsp. pepper

I medium-sized potato

1½ c. vegetable oil

*See recipe on page 39 for tips on cleaning and deveining fresh shrimp.

1. Wash and dry shrimp and place half of them in a food processor or blender. Process until pastelike. Cut the rest of the shrimp in half the long way and set aside.

2. Place flour in a large bowl and gradually stir in water until batter is smooth. Add salt, pepper, and shrimp paste, and stir well.

3. Peel potato and cut into very thin shoestrings. Add to batter and stir.

4. Heat oil over high heat in a wok or a deep saucepan. Place about 2 tbsp. of batter in a ladle or deep serving spoon. Place half a shrimp in the middle of the ladle and carefully drop the batter and shrimp into the hot oil.

5. Fry for about 1 minute and turn over. Fry until batter is golden and shrimp is pink, about 3 minutes.

6. Remove from oil, drain on paper towel, and set aside. Repeat with remaining batter and shrimp and serve with nuoc cham.

Preparation time: 20 to 25 minutes
Cooking time: 1 hour
Serves 4 to 6

New Year's Cake / Banh chung

No Tet celebration is complete without this special rice cake. Although it takes a long time to prepare, the final product is well worth the effort.

2 c. sticky rice

¼ c. dried mung beans, hulled

6 oz. boneless pork shoulder or roast, cut into ¼-inch slices

2 tbsp. green onions, chopped

1½ tbsp. fish sauce

½ tsp. pepper

¼ tsp. salt

1½ tbsp. vegetable oil

1 c. water

plastic wrap

aluminum foil

string

1. Place rice in one bowl and mung beans in another. Cover each with water and soak overnight.*

2. In a large bowl, combine pork, onions, fish sauce, and pepper. Set aside for 30 minutes.

3. While pork mixture is marinating, drain rice and beans thoroughly. Add salt to rice and stir well.

4. In a skillet or wok, heat oil over medium heat. Add pork mixture and stir-fry until meat is cooked through but still tender, about 4 to 6 minutes. Remove from heat and set aside.

5. In a medium saucepan, combine mung beans and about 1 c. water. Simmer over low heat for 20 minutes, or until soft. Remove from heat, drain, and mash beans with a potato masher or fork.

6. On a countertop, spread out a piece of plastic wrap about 17 inches square. On top of this, place a sheet of aluminum foil of the same size. Place almost half of the sticky rice in the middle of the foil and shape rice into a square layer.

7. Top rice with a layer of beans, using half of them. Place pork slices on top of beans. Add remaining beans and top off with most of the remaining rice.

8. Wrap cake by bringing together two edges of foil and plastic wrap. Fold edges over twice and flatten against the side of the packet.

9. Tuck remaining rice into the two open ends of the packet, covering up beans and meat. Fold the open ends as if you were wrapping a gift. Place packet, folded side down, on another large sheet of plastic wrap and wrap tightly. Tie securely with a long piece of heavy string or twine, lengthwise and crosswise. The packet should be square or rectangular.

10. Place packet in a large stockpot full of water and bring to a boil. Reduce heat and simmer uncovered for 4 hours, adding water if necessary. Remove from heat and cool for 1 hour.

11. To serve, slice wrapped packet into 4 slices. Unwrap, arrange on a plate, and serve.

When traditional banh chung is prepared in Vietnam, the rice absorbs a slight green color from the banana leaves in which the cakes are wrapped. If you'd like a little color in your dish, simply add a drop of green food coloring to the rice and water before leaving to soak.

*Preparation time: 45 to 55 minutes
(plus overnight soaking)
Cooking time: 4¾ hours, plus 1 hour to cool
Serves 4*

Fresh Fruit Salad / Trai cay

Vietnam's many varieties of fresh fruit are popular offerings to the ancestors on festive occasions. A light dressing adds extra flavor to this simple dish.

6 servings of fresh fruit*

⅔ c. lime juice

3 tbsp. honey

½ tsp. sesame oil

1 tsp. ground cinnamon

pinch of salt

1. Cut fruit into bite-sized pieces and place in a large bowl.

2. Place lime juice in a medium-sized bowl and gradually stir in honey. The mixture should be smooth and creamy. Add sesame oil, cinnamon, and salt, and stir well.

3. Pour dressing over fruit and mix gently. Place in the refrigerator for 15 minutes.

4. Serve in individual bowls.

Preparation time: 15 to 20 minutes
Chilling time: 15 minutes
Serves 6

*You may choose to serve just one kind of fruit or an assortment for this dish. Choose ripe, brightly colored specimens of whatever is in season. A few favorite varieties in Vietnam are bananas, mangoes, melons, and star fruit.

Fresh fruit salad is as delicious as it is colorful. It makes a great snack or a perfect dessert for any meal! For a little extra color, garnish with a sprig of fresh mint.

Index

About the Author

Chi Nguyen was born near Hanoi, Vietnam, and with her family moved to Ho Chi Minh City (formerly Saigon), Vietnam, in 1954. Nguyen graduated from the University of Saigon School of Pharmacy, and she and her family left Vietnam in 1975. As a resident of Minneapolis, Minnesota, Nguyen enjoys cooking native Vietnamese dishes for her family and friends.

Judy Monroe, born in Duluth, Minnesota, learned Vietnamese cooking while in high school and mastered several Southeast Asian cuisines. A graduate of the University of Minnesota, Monroe has worked as a biomedical librarian and a freelance writer. In her spare time, she enjoys ethnic cooking, baking, gardening, and reading.

Photo acknowledgements
The photographs in this book are reproduced courtesy of: © Nevada Wier, pp. 2–3, 11, 14; © Walter, Louiseann Pietrowicz/September 8th Stock, pp. 4 (left), 5 (both), 6, 18, 30, 35, 44, 49, 50, 53, 54, 58, 62, 69; © Robert L. & Diane Wolfe, pp. 4 (right), 36, 40, 43, 61; © John Elk III, p. 26.

Cover photos: © Robert L. & Diane Wolfe (all).

The illustrations on pp. 7, 19, 27, 29, 31, 33, 34, 37, 38, 39, 41, 42, 45, 48, 51, 55, 56, 57, 63, 64, 65, 67, and 68 and the map on p. 8 are by Tim Seeley.